EVERYTHING
IS MENTAL

NIKOLAOS PALOUMBIS

ISBN: 978-0-578-33829-3

CONTENTS

CHAPTER 1

STAY SHARP AND FOCUSED

IF YOU ASK A SUCCESSFUL person how they achieved the title of being "successful," you get an answer along the lines of "Overcoming my fears and believing in myself."

But did they always naturally have the ability to believe in themselves? Or did they start from scratch? If so, then where exactly did they start?

The key is to start. Commence. Begin. *Try*, because it all starts with an **action**.

Giving up is not even a thought.

It can become challenging to stay motivated amidst all the disappointments, but the journey that I am going to take you on will hopefully help you understand self-realization and improvement. You won't need to do much. You will simply have to look for the things you already possess. I will teach you about a heuristic approach to life. It will lead to self-discovery, self-optimization, and robust decision-making. All in all, it will enable you to not give up when everything is falling apart.

We'll start by taking lessons from our failures. A failure leads to two possibilities: either you give up and lose hope, or you start anew with much more knowledge than before.

Let's face it: we've all been a victim of failure. But despite the letdowns and botched plans, be persistent and make the best of your situation. Despite the roadblocks, believe in your strength and keep going. Remember, you're in the position you're in regardless, so focus, and enhance what's working.

Being alive in the moment

Think about the path you are on. It's truly remarkable that you got up today and took action! It's extraordinary that you can be positive in the face of adversity, and amazingly, you have the privilege of going through life moment by moment. So, take a deep breath and look at things from a different perspective. Even if you have to force yourself to be positive, smile. It is an option, and it is contagious.

Being ourselves

Be your true self unapologetically, and do not hide behind the curtains of stability and consistency. Do not be afraid of following your heart and listening to your gut. Even though many people will tell you to do this, what they won't say is this: *Do not believe the bad reviews, and certainly learn not to believe the good ones.*

Nobody in this world knows you better than you do. You know what you do in the dark when no one's looking, what you think about when you get lost in thought, and what you feel in your heart. Don't let anyone derail you from your path, and don't listen to anyone's opinions of you—even the good ones. As a matter of fact, you'll receive advice all day long from anyone and everyone. However, your job is to not listen to those who have never done what you want to do.

Verify everything.

They say, "Believe none of what you hear, and half of what you see." I say, believe nothing; verify everything. Do not believe everything you see on the Internet and in the media. Here is an example. Today, you read your horoscope and learned that you should be cautious of relationships. What will you do? Not get into a new relationship because some psychic told you not to? No. You will heed their advice, but not become a slave of their opinion; you will do what *you* think is best for you.

Do not adjust to a situation until you are satisfied with where you are. If things are becoming jumbled up, remember to take your time and break them down to build yourself back up. Also, don't live a mediocre life only because it doesn't challenge you. Embrace the challenge, tweak it, and evolve according to it.

We often think that things will be hard to do, but it only requires a small action: starting. Once you develop the courage to just begin, the rest becomes easier to do. It isn't easy to start, I know. But trust me, the feeling is liberating. I believe that we all have the potential to make diamonds out of coal.

Think of it this way: You're facing a failure and are in a slump. So, what will giving up get you? You will still face your failure in the morning, you will still be living the same old boring lifestyle that you hate, and you will always be judged. Nothing will change. But what if you change your mindset? Look at things from a different perspective, and you will find hidden opportunities in your failures, a way to learn and move ahead. The only thing you can do after you fall is get back up! Through hard work, dedication, and commitment, you can change your path.

You need to understand that *nothing changes if nothing changes.* You're going to remain in the same position regardless, so why not take a chance? If you're going to give up and lose hope, it will keep happening again and again. You might think to yourself, *I will do better next time,* but the next time will not be any better unless you make a change.

People have delusional beliefs that if they have failed the first few times, they will never succeed. You could be right on the cusp of success, but you are restricted by your negative thoughts. I say that if you want to indulge in a thought, why not make it a positive one? Before you think that you might fail *again,* make it a habit to think that you might succeed this time. We've all been there; we've all been discouraged by failures. But what we have to see is that we *are* succeeding, even if it doesn't seem like we are at the time. There is no destination; the process itself is the destination. When you arrive where you've never been before, there will be a new destination to reach.

The series of "what ifs" are only going to drive you crazy if you don't give it a shot. What if you had accepted that offer? What if you had chosen a different career? What if you hadn't given up…? The thought and energy that you waste in your life can easily be applied to pursuing your passion. It will also save you years of regret and resentment. Think about the consequences before giving up.

Just take the first step. Start by creating a checklist of your most essential tasks, and think of things your heart most desires to do. Whether it's writing a book, creating a song, or even building a skyscraper, start by writing that first sentence, composing that first lyric, or making that first sketch, and the rest will follow. Word by word, note by note, block by block, your dreams will come to fruition.

Confidence will come from keeping the promises you make to yourself.

More suffering is caused by imagination than by reality. Start small; progress can be contagious. Long-term problems call for short-term solutions. So, create short-term goals for yourself, and celebrate your successes. Find your anchor: it can be your friends, family, or even yourself. Find the thing that keeps you grounded and humble, and stay accountable. Your mentor is the future version of yourself.

Listen to yourself.

Don't care what others think and say, and don't let the opinions of other people hold you back. People will always criticize; it's in their nature. Don't let criticism stop you, either. Embrace it and turn it into motivation instead. Great ideas are often met with great criticism. You will never be criticized by someone who is doing more than you—only by those who are doing less. Most people will not even support you until they see you achieving your dreams. Decide what it is you love, and commit to it. Distractions will separate you from your goals and the life you want, so cut off any distractions and stay focused. Consistently execute your plans, and you'll succeed.

Tap into your inner energy. You have the strength to lift entire mountains; you only have to find it. Find the things that make you smile, and use them to create positive energy in your life.

Procrastinating is one of the most comfortable things you can do. Comfort is a drug. Don't become addicted; start moving. They say, "Good things come to those who wait." I say, great things come to those who *don't* wait! Life is too short to wait. "He not busy being born is busy dying." Don't wait for the motivation to start. Start, and the motivation will come. It's amazing what we can do when we just start to do it. If you never try, you'll never know. You don't have to be an expert before you get started. You don't even have to be ready to start. Just take the first step. You're ready. Start now.

CHAPTER 2

EVERYTHING IS MENTAL

THROUGHOUT MY JOURNEY, I HAVE collected many pieces of advice, tips, and inspirational anecdotes that have helped me reach where I am today. This book is a collection of those anecdotes, and I share them with you because I believe they will benefit any reader and enable you to become a better version of yourself.

Perception of reality is more real than reality itself.

When people hear me say this, they usually don't understand what it means. It means that every situation and experience in our lives is clouded by our perception of it. For instance, you might see x when in reality it's y; you're just assuming that it's x without actually digging any deeper. Reality is fleeting; it's all in our heads. But here's the good news: if it's all in our heads, and we can change a y into an x in our minds, we can also turn it back into a y. If it is within our ability to focus on the worst and think the worst, it is also in our ability to look at the silver lining and the best possible outcome. In the end, it is your mindset that determines your outcome.

How you do anything is how you do everything.

Our habits dictate our future. The decisions that we make—whether it's how we dress, how we talk, how we move, or how we think—have a tendency to extend into our future. Everything that we do in a day will determine how things go the next day. Let's say you start your Monday with a healthy breakfast and exercise. Not only is your day going to be productive and energetic, it will also motivate you to start Tuesday the same way. Energy is contagious.

On the other hand, if you wake up twenty minutes late for your important meeting on Monday and go to work with that same mindset, your Tuesday will be spent catching up on Monday's missed work. Hence, our comfort is correlated with our reality. Once you get comfortable, that reality sets where you are mentally— and how that will determine your outcome. Therefore, don't get comfortable. Strive for more. Anything is possible. Get comfortable with being uncomfortable.

Who you mimic is who you become.

If you must mimic somebody, mimic the better version of yourself that you wish to be. Imitate the person that you want to be in the future, and start today. Once you begin mimicking that person, people start viewing you as that person, and the reality of you being that person slowly comes to fruition.

So, mimic the person you want to be, and once you become that person, strive to become an even bigger and better version of yourself. Every day that you mimic yourself, you transition into the person you want to be, and that never changes. You will keep growing until you reach a better place. When you do, aim for an even better place, and your mindset will start changing too. Whether you know it or not, your mindset says a lot about you. People understand where you stand in life based on how you perceive things.

Your opinion is usually related to your experience and income.

Everyone has opinions in this world, and for most people, those opinions are based on how much they really know about the things they're giving their opinions on.

As you start gaining more experience, your perceptions and opinions change. You will look at things from a different perspective and understand them much better. Experience also opens our eyes to a better understanding of the decisions and opinions of other people. As a kid, you may have looked at the antagonist in a movie and determined that they were the "villain," but as you grew up and experienced the world, you started comprehending what the antagonist meant, and you may have even related to them more.

Similarly, money shapes our opinions. When you start earning more money, it usually translates to you having more experience, leading to a different perspective. So, your opinion coincides with your income and experience. Your perception of money will determine how much you earn.

The less you complain, the bigger your dreams.

If you're complaining about the small hindrances and obstacles in your path, you're not looking at the bigger picture. Understand that what you're complaining about today is not even close to how it's going to be once you have progressed. You're letting some tiny little thing mess with your mindset in that specific moment, rather than looking at the bigger picture and realizing it's irrelevant. Don't complain just knowing that something unfavorable could potentially happen. You will essentially stress yourself out over something that is likely to happen. Taking that approach would be counterproductive. If you're genuinely determined and motivated, you will not complain about obstacles. Instead, you will face them head-on and let them improve you.

Everyone has opinions; follow the actual influence.

With the changing times, it's becoming difficult to separate fact from fiction. Everyone seems to have an opinion, and spoken words and rumors manifest themselves as the truth. Don't believe everything you think. To become successful, you must find the distinction between what's real and what's opinion. For instance, if someone is doing something and the media proclaims they have all the information, follow the facts. Don't have a whatever-the-media-portrays mindset. False knowledge is more dangerous than ignorance. Imagine how many people may dislike you because they didn't hear your side of the story. The worst thing is when people get targeted when they've done nothing wrong. The media is infamous for selling stories that trigger the feelings of those who question nothing. People make speculative assertions disguised as fact, with minimal knowledge. Their perception of you is a reflection of them, and your reaction to them is an awareness of you. Hence, don't follow people's opinions. Forget them, their opinions, and their thoughts.

Playing it small does not serve the world.

For me, writing this book was a hugely necessary step. I wanted to tell people to dream of bigger and better things, and I wanted to change their perspective. If I told all of this to one person, it could start a chain reaction that could help many people. But imagine how many people can start thinking bigger when they hear my experience indirectly, without ever meeting me. For me to be able to become the best version of myself, I need to constantly keep upgrading myself internally. For that to happen, I need to experience more, understand better, and improve my mentality overall.

The biggest asset we have is our mindset, and the most important commodity we have is our time. It is the only thing we'll never get back. The worst thing we can do with our time is assume we'll have more. For me to get more time, I need to live longer. For that to be possible, I need to live a healthier life. I need to be the least stressed version of myself for that to be accomplished. I need to eat as healthy as possible and be in my best shape at all times. I could help one person in one day, but my service to this world will simultaneously help many other people through this book. We all need to take steps that will serve the world on a much larger scale.

Excellence has no age limit.

You could be a child prodigy, but you could also excel in your craft at an old age. Excellence is not limited by age. It can be achieved as a four-year-old or as a forty-year-old. The key is your mindset. Do not give up before trying your hardest, and even then, do not give up *after* trying your hardest. You can become a master of your craft through practice and preparation. Your ambition should be limitless. You have unlimited potential.

Thoughts influence action.

Your thoughts create your imagination. If you wish to change your reality, you need to first change your mindset. Reality is created by the mind. If you realized how powerful your thoughts are, you would never think negatively again.

One way to handle pressure is to apply it.

Sometimes people get overwhelmed by high stakes and expectations (our own and others'), but you should not let yourself get crushed under pressure. We must embrace it and apply it to make it a driving force for us. Just keep doing it, and as with the trickle effect, things will start happening.

Have goals so big, you feel uncomfortable telling closed-minded people.

We're all here to play a different role in life, but what I want is for you to take center stage and create a goal so big that closed-minded people won't even understand it. Say you want to be an opera singer, a billionaire, or a world-class basketball player. Reach for the stars. If others have done it, so can you. For every reason why "it's not possible," there are thousands of people who have faced the same circumstances—and succeeded. However, don't resent other people's success; celebrate it. Understand that if someone else can do or achieve something, so can you, for nothing is beyond possible. Everything is easy; getting started is the hardest part. Disconnect from negative energy. Focus. Create such big goals for yourself that explaining them to people who do not share the same mental perspective as you becomes an uncomfortable experience. Those that understand you will be attracted to you like magnets.

Why do people give up?

People give up because they expect quick results. They

fear the future. They feel the world owes them something. They get overworked and burned out. They fear failure more than they desire success. They stop believing in themselves. They resist change and are inflexible. They get stuck in the past. They give up their power. They never visualize what is possible. They see failure as a signal to turn back. They feel sorry for themselves. They feel they have something to lose. They believe in their weaknesses. They dwell on mistakes. The list goes on and on and on. Let me tell you that this is not the behavior of a successful and strong-minded person. So, if any of these behaviors apply to you, you should change your mindset and use it to increase your power.

Fear of failure leads to failure.

The fear of losing keeps you from winning. When you take risks—calculated risks—in order to achieve your dreams and desires, those risks are not taken in vain. Take risks in life. Even if you lose, you always learn something. Most people don't even try. At least you won't have the regret of knowing you never tried. Once you realize how necessary it is to take risks in order to grow, you'll deliberately take risks. If you don't, you'll end up helping others take their risks.

Having a plan B ensures failure.

There is no such thing as a plan B. If you go into something with the idea that if you fail, you'll just move on to plan B, then plan B becomes plan A. Your subconscious mind remains focused on plan B. You don't realize it, but in knowing there's another option if you fail, you get comfortable not putting one hundred percent of your effort towards the main goal.

You get what you focus on, so focus on what you want.

If you look at your past, you will see how everything has to led you to your current situation. So, if you are happy financially, physically, and emotionally, it's because you took steps in the past that led to this moment. Think about it this way: the steps you take today will impact your future. If you don't envision your future, you'll just relive your past. Be loyal to your future, not your past. Don't let your future self down by complaining and being stagnant in the present. Don't make excuses. Take steps for a better future. Ensure that you are transitioning into a person that your future self will be proud of.

Surround yourself with those who have the same mission as you.

There's a difference between being smart and being educated. If a person is educated, they have knowledge and a good grasp of certain subjects or topics. However, if they are smart or intelligent, they can use that information and benefit themselves by applying it to their lives. Being smart is about how you act on information. People need to stop worrying about what school they've graduated from as a determining factor of their intelligence. Dismissing someone's understanding of a topic based on what grade they received or what school they attended is beyond ridiculous and narrow-minded. Education doesn't have to mean going to college. This isn't to discourage anyone from getting an education or good grades. Specific professions require this, and it's a good exercise to attain people skills. However, "graduating" in the real world is your real degree. There's a difference between education and wisdom.

Surrounding yourself with people who have the

same goals and objectives as you will give you positive reinforcement and guidance. It's important to know that accepting help from other people does not make you inferior; in fact, choosing the right advice and implementing it in your life is a sign of intelligence. Mentality is everything, and the right balance will move you forward.

Better a little caution than a large regret.

You have to learn to play your cards right. In this case, practice is vital, and learning to enhance your natural instinct is paramount. Human beings have a *gut feeling* or *intuition,* and it is not something to be ignored. What we call "intuition" is actually a predictive processing framework in our brains that ensures the ability to deal with unpredictable situations easily.

> *We are what we repeatedly do. Excellence then is not an act, but a habit.*
> —Aristotle

When you have sufficient experience or practice in a given field, the brain becomes trained to predict your the outcomes of your actions. Thus, a "gut feeling" is actually a result of our programming. When a person follows an instinct and becomes cautious, they are actually listening to their programmed brains. That is why you should create a habit of listening, pondering, and reviewing a situation before making a concrete decision.

It pays to move quickly and decisively when the time is right.

It may seem difficult or arduous, but when we develop the habit of making the right decisions, making the right moves, and moving with the right choices, it starts coming naturally. At first it seems like rocket science, until you develop a better understanding. Practice makes perfect. The more you practice, the better you get at whatever it is you are doing, resulting in the understanding that everything is easy, it's just hard at first.

These are the ways human beings essentially train their minds to think quicker, faster, and more reliably. Making the right moves quickly and at the right time will also become second nature as we work hard, practice, and think. There are no physical limitations as long as we have the right mentality.

It's okay to live a life others don't understand.

Not everyone in life will think the same way, have the same experiences, or share the same opinions. We look at things from our own perspectives, and our life experiences impact our decision-making. One thing I can say I've verified over time is that common sense is not so common. People will criticize your way if it doesn't fit with their perception, but that doesn't make them right—nor does it make you wrong. It only makes them different. And it's okay to think differently; in fact, it's recommended.

Being different is not a problem. In fact, it's the solution. Life becomes more colorful when people step out of their comfort zone and embrace the path of their dreams. So don't be afraid to stand out. Stay firm on your opinions, and dare to be unique.

Replace "I wish" with "I will."

You don't get what you wish for; you get what you work for. Wishful thinking is tenuous. Wishful planning, however, will be fruitful. When you replace "I wish" with "I will," it will make your brain work more productively.

For instance, you may say, "I wish I had a million dollars," and then go to sleep. Or you could replace it with "I *will* have a million dollars," and now you have a plan. Go further and think, "I will have a million dollars if ___," and your brain will start to slowly finish the sentence. Whether it is by working that much harder, complaining that much less, improving *x*, changing *y*, etc., the word *if* is a huge word, even though it's only two letters.

Soon, you will start programming your brain to replace wishful thinking with wishful planning. Your brain has the power to make you poor or rich, and the way you tilt your scales is right here: in your mind.

The heaviest burdens that we carry are the thoughts in our heads.

For you to run at your highest capacity, you'll need to consume at the highest capacity—not just what you eat or drink, but how you think. There is nothing that can trouble you more than overthinking. Our minds are very powerful; through our minds, we can either achieve our greatest goals or put ourselves in a mental prison. It is in our hands. A failure or mishap is nothing to be afraid of; it is what will make you successful the next time. Our brains are our most powerful tools. They are the fastest, and most efficient processors in existence. Constantly clearing out the cache keeps our computers running fast. Similarly, clearing out our thoughts also removes the burden from the mind. It is good to learn from your mistakes, but becoming trapped inside them is a mistake you cannot afford.

Planning leads to victory.

People assume that success and accomplishment are limited only to gifted or blessed people. They associate "luck" with planning, working hard, falling, getting back up, and not giving up. Success comes from planning out every move you make. It may fall into people's laps unexpectedly, but it can only be sustained when dealt with strategically and mindfully. Setting short-term goals will help achieve long-term goals. It is the smart thing to do. And the anticipation of the next steps makes the journey worthwhile.

If you can't change your mind, then you can't change anything.

Mentality is everything. Our mind controls our actions, emotions, and thoughts. Until you change your thinking, you'll keep recycling your experiences. Control your emotions, or be consumed by them. Too many people fall victim to this. Don't let emotion get in the way of the true pursuit of what matters in being successful. Embrace change and welcome challenges. You have to train your mind to be stronger than your emotions, or else you'll lose yourself every time. Doing something over and over again and expecting different results is the definition of insanity. If you keep getting the same results, it is time to change the approach.

Change your negative thoughts to positive ones. Change what you dream about. Change your habits. Change what you read. Change your friends. Change how you see yourself. Some people will judge you for changing; others will celebrate you for growing. Then there are those who can see through the bullshit, and those who can't. Don't squander your limited time here with those who can't.

Changing your mentality in order to better adapt

to the environment is vital for success. Your brain is a muscle. People who are not so open-minded see things negatively. The more open-minded you become, the more you start to see things positively. Once you understand that your mentality is everything, you can shift your mind to think and act accordingly. Your attitude towards life determines life's attitude towards you.

Accentuate the positive. Eliminate the negative.

Personal growth requires consistent input of positivity. Avoid any negative energy coming your way. Don't waste any energy on things you cannot control.

You attract what you want to attract.

When a person thinks positively, they attract and manifest positivity in their lives. Similarly, when a person thinks negatively, even positive things look negative to them, and they become pessimistic. They are training their minds to find the one negative thing in the pile of positivity. When people want to lose weight, they immediately think of diets. No such thing as going on a diet, period! You need to start living healthier. Stop pointing your finger at those who actually took the steps to live healthy. Quit saying things like "I wish I looked like that" or "I'll never look like that." Instead, say, "I *will* look like that," then follow through with the necessary steps. The healthier the meal, the better it starts tasting. Start living a healthy lifestyle. When you put in the *effort,* you will enjoy the fruits of your hard work.

Don't advise those who don't ask for it.

You are doing yourself a disservice when you advise those who don't want it. Their actions and thoughts are constrained by their minds. Human beings can do anything. Everything becomes easy when we decide to change. Don't entertain those who don't wish to learn, because when we decide to change our current situation, that is when things start to move in the right direction. So don't give this advice to someone who is not ready for that change; only give advice to those who ask for it. Unless someone wants to change themselves for the better, there's nothing you can do to change that person. If you correct a fool, they'll feel offended. But if you correct a wise person, they'll appreciate it.

Your mentality defines you.

It all comes down to this: *everything is mental*. The mind contains the strength to tackle a million problems, carry a billion boulders, and climb the highest walls. You just have to take the first step. Make the right choices. Play it smart. Think about everything. Review your mistakes. Don't back down after a failure. Sustain your success through progress. Turn practices into habits, and make them second nature. Grow with the time. Have a positive mindset. Don't complain. Try to be the person you see yourself as in the future. This is what will make you successful. This is your key to success. This is what will create excellence in everything you do. Your mindset is all, and your mind is everything.

CHAPTER 3

LOGIC OVER EMOTION

LET'S FOCUS ON THE LOGICAL aspects of the brain. *Everything is Mental* is about eradicating the concept of "I can't do it, it's impossible," and replacing it with the knowledge gained by overcoming those fears and triumphing over the challenges one faces.

Humans are emotional.

When a person faces a problem, the logical first step is to analyze it and formulate a plan to move ahead. However, what happens is that demotivation and discouragement trap them into a loop of self-loathing. What people don't realize—or only realize too late—is that they will remain stuck in that place if they stay stagnant and don't move forward. They will remain trapped in the loop of despair; their situation will not change. But if they take steps towards finding a solution, they will manifest a solution or encourage their brains to find a way out of the problem. Focus on using the logical part of the mind to find solutions to life's problems.

Good news is temporary, but bad news drags.

The reason people forget the good news and focus on the bad is that the latter has a deeper impact on their brains. For instance, if a lawyer has two cases in a day, and they win one and lose the other, they will focus on the one they lost more than the one they won. However, if they only focused on the win—and indeed, learned from the loss—then things would be more constructive. Perception is everything; you cannot let yourself down because of the negative. In the end, perception also impacts other endeavors and people in life.

Don't look for approval.

People always criticize, comment, and have an opinion.

It's important to keep doing what you're doing and not look to others for approval. Do whatever makes you happy, and chase your happiness in spite of the naysayers. For instance, if you want to become a painter, and people tell you that it's not a viable option, don't listen to them. Focus on your happiness and motivation and follow your dreams.

Learn everything about something, and something about everything.

The problem is not the problem. The problem is your attitude about the problem. The primary cause of unhappiness is not the situation, but rather how you react to it. If you don't understand something, don't just dismiss it like the majority in the world does. Knowledge dispels fear. Don't be dismissive of or negative towards things that you don't fundamentally understand. Most people, when they don't understand something, disparage it. Don't be like most people; get to understand it. Knowledge is power.

Bring out the solution, not the emotion.

You're going to be stuck in a situation regardless, so why not take steps to get out of the problem? Either you can become demotivated and think, *Why me?* or you can take a step back, draw a few breaths, and try to find a way out. Rather than focusing on the negative aspects, look at the silver lining. Engage your logical side and think, *How can I fix this?* Make it a habit to focus on a solution rather than focusing on the problem.

Train your mind to be calm in every situation.

On the road, when a person narrowly escapes an accident, it is a sign of a good driver if they do not get flustered or engage in road rage. Similarly, remaining calm and being logical is an indication of a person with strong mental capabilities. The good news is that this behavior is not a natural talent; it is a learned technique. Therefore, you can learn it too. Practice remaining calm in the face of adversity, take a few breaths, analyze the problem from the opposite perspective, form a mental plan, and then approach the issue.

Regurgitating unoriginal information

How many times has it happened that you saw the news online or read something and formed your opinion in your mind ... but when you saw the public's opinion, it made you change your own? Your original opinion—the one that you had from the beginning—was unique, and you should never suppress that. Straying from the herd, being the black sheep, and not following the crowd is an impressive quality, and it should be encouraged. Thinking is difficult; that's why you'll see most people judge. You need to get all the facts before you come up with a conclusion. Start by considering the context. Critical thinking is crucial when forming opinions and making decisions, so don't just agree with everyone simply to be part of the group. Take a chance and become your own unique individual.

You have to know the difference between naïve aggression and effective aggression.

If you are stuck in a difficult situation and not making any progress, ask yourself, "What am I doing wrong, why is my situation not changing, and how can I make a difference?" Answering these questions will give you insight into the immobility of your circumstances. Sitting on the couch and shouting at the wall will not do you any good. You need to take that aggression and use it to light the fire of your passion. That is what I call "effective aggression."

How smart you are is determined by how you respond or react to the information you receive.

Being smart is knowing when you don't have enough information to evaluate something. It is understanding that there are more pieces to the puzzle, and once you have obtained them, understanding that there are still more to obtain. It's better to have questions that can't be answered than answers that can be questioned. Examine a court case and how they break it down from every angle, so you can understand it and see it from a different perspective. Opinion is gathered from personal experience and information we've collected. Facts are irrefragable.

There's more in the context than what we perceive with our emotions.

Too many people make impulsive decisions based on limited information. Intelligence is the ability to challenge everything you know. In order for you to learn, you need to challenge your own ideas. You must always be willing to truly consider evidence that contradicts your beliefs and admit the possibility that you may be wrong.

An opinion may be considered a statement of fact if that fact exists. In deciding this issue, you should consider whether the average listener would conclude, from the language of a statement and its context, that the person is making a statement of fact. There is an issue here: What happens when two people perceive the same thing differently? If your perception of a given event doesn't line up with someone else's, whose perception of that event is true? Most people try to uncover facts that support their perception. Try and seek the absolute truth, even if it contradicts your beliefs. Embracing the possibility that a different perception is more factual is encouraging growth within yourself.

It is better to see something once than to hear about it a thousand times.

Life is about taking chances, being adventurous, and following your desires. The most exhilarating part of life is when you feel the rush of excitement in your blood from following your dreams. So why not take that chance? Be resilient in your pursuit of happiness. Don't miss out on opportunities because of fear or discomfort; embrace them. Even if you get burned a little, you will become stronger. And instead of hearing about things from others, you will experience it for yourself.

True power is restraint. Challenge your impulse.

High-status people are nonreactive. They don't have emotional outbursts. They understand how to stay calm in any situation, interpret the scenario, then respond accordingly—but never emotionally. You will continue to suffer if you have an emotional reaction to everything that is said to you. For instance, it may be your first impulse to argue with someone who is criticizing your work, but as previously mentioned, people always have an opinion. Your true power lies in sitting back and observing things from a logical perspective. Most people make decisions based on their emotions. Those who understand this are the ones who pull the strings to trigger those who act upon their emotions. Your outcomes result from how you respond to news, and how you respond to news tells the world where you stand mentally. Don't let opinions or words control you, because if you do, that means everyone else can control you. A wise person never argues with those who can't yet see their vision.

Silence is more powerful than proving a point.

A smart person knows what to say, but a wise person knows whether or not to say it. The less that people think, the louder they tend to be. Knowing what to say and knowing whether you should say it are two different things. It is better to be at peace in silence than to argue with people who don't understand your ideas. Sometimes it takes a while for people to embrace your genius. As the saying goes, "The world is not ready for your vision yet." People who don't have the same vision as you will never understand why you work so hard or distance yourself from others. Why bother arguing over dissimilarities when you can quietly observe your piece of art? A smart person avoids an argument because they already know there will not be any resolution. You don't have to attend every argument you're invited to. Sometimes it's best to just disconnect and walk away. The best revenge is getting yourself to a place where you no longer care about revenge. They say, "Weak people seek revenge, strong people forgive, and intelligent people ignore." Be strong and intelligent.

Don't try to find the black and white in the grey area.

Most things in this world are not black and white. Whether you call them a blessing or a curse, new inventions and innovations in recent years have also opened up people's minds. Nothing is all right or wrong, people are not all good or evil, and situations are not always black and white. So, for instance, if a person comes to you and asks for your opinion, do not fall prey to the *opinion of the majority*; find your own answer. See the situation in shades of grey. If you weren't directly involved in the situation, don't form an opinion based on what you hear.

The truth sounds like hate to those that hate the truth.

My answer to this would be "I don't have enough information to give an opinion." It's easier to sell someone than to let them know they're being sold. For most people, their understanding is limited and thus more easily swayed in giving their perception a reality. The price you pay for something is as much as you don't know about it. The less you know, the more you can and will be fooled. The biggest downfall of a person, nation, or society is the belief that their opinion—or someone else's—is the absolute truth. When people lose their tolerance and close their minds to others' points of view, it makes them stagnant. Change and enhancement cannot come to a stagnant mind. There is a difference between an opinion and a fact. An opinion is formed after information has been collected, leading to a better understanding of a situation, while a fact is immutable; it does not change, and it's universal. Unlike a fact, an opinion can enhance and improve upon the collection of new data.

The world needs more rationality and less rationalizing. Rationalizing is searching for justification after you've already reached an opinion or decision. Rationality is seeking the best logic and data before you commit, and staying open to changing your mind.

Study your goal.

Consider others who are in the position you're soon to be in, and observe their attitudes and mindset. The less you understand something, the less you should dismiss it. Get to understand it. If you want to be a pianist, read the autobiographies of the pioneers in your field. If you want to be a chess master, go over all the games played by the highest-ranked chess players in the world. Absorb information daily from various sources to expand your knowledge and understanding of their motivations, struggles, and best and worst moments. It will give you a head start on facing the problems in your field, open your eyes to the prejudices and problems these people face, and help you strive to overcome those problems.

Perspective is everything.

Everything is mental, and our perspective is shaped by our mentality and understanding. It is in our ability to look at the positive, and it is in our ability to gloom over the negative. We choose the narrative we wish to listen to. The world could be telling you "This is a good thing" or "This is your best option," but if you disagree because you don't think it is, then nothing else matters. Your perspective is what moves you forward, or it is what holds you back. If you think logically and analyze a situation, it might lead to a different perspective. It is also logical to look at the opposite perspective, as it will help you to either form a different point of view or improve the one you already have.

It's all relevant to your mindset.

Mentality is everything. You can choose to make something relevant or irrelevant. The mindset, opinions, and viewpoints you garner are the determining factors in the relevance of a situation. If you believe or decide that *these things don't matter,* they will not stay pertinent.

Focus on the silver lining.

Ask yourself, "What is good in this situation?" Now focus on that. We form a habit of always looking at the bad side of our circumstances, thinking about our losses, and focusing on the darkness that engulfs us. BUT, if we choose to look at the positive side of things, what we learned from our losses, and the silver lining on the dark clouds, it will take us out of negativity and pessimism. Negative thoughts are unconstructive and unhelpful, and by choosing to engage in them, you are missing out on the chance to make things better. Instead, you can take a breath, give yourself time to think, and focus on constructive and productive thoughts.

Don't trust easy sales pitches.

As they say, "Life is not a bed of roses." Anyone who tells you that they can change your life in just a few days is probably selling you false dreams. Don't allow yourself to be moved by voices that speak only to your anger or frustration. Don't let them take advantage of your bad day, because that's when you are most vulnerable. Life is a struggle; it is not all gold and rainbows, and there are going to be dark days with rain. But that is what makes it worthwhile, because struggle is temporary.

Sacrifices are like investments: give up short-term comfort for a long-term win. Those dark days improve us; they mold us into stronger people. You should not be afraid of failures or problems. Embrace them, knowing that they will make you better—and that they will end. After all, good things do take time. The first step in moving to where you want to be is to stop wishing to be in the position you're in.

CHAPTER 4

SUCCESS

PART 1: Hustle

PEOPLE ARE ALWAYS LOOKING FOR a formula to making a quick buck. It is natural: you see people you graduated with making more than you, and you immediately yearn to make a lot more, and at a quicker pace. Perhaps you see a colleague getting paid more merely because they got there before you. Isn't it frustrating knowing that someone is in a higher position than you simply because they came earlier? You might think that they don't deserve it. But guess what? They didn't keep you from applying for the job before they did; they got there early because you came in late. That's it. Call it a formula maybe, but moving one step forward when no one else will, getting up early, and applying to every opportunity you find—that's hustling. That is precisely what will get you a better job, better pay, and the life that you have planned for yourself.

Great things come to those who don't wait.

Consider this: You are on your spring or summer break. How would you utilize this time? Of course, you would go on a family vacation. You labored all semester, and you need some time off to relax. Then, about three weeks into your vacation, you realize it's been days since you last picked up a book or did any studying. You're relaxed, and you don't have care in the world. What do you do now? Do you spend the next month of your break doing the same thing, or do you get up and look for an opportunity to move ahead? The answer to this question will tell you if you're going to be complaining about your paycheck for the rest of your life, or if you'll be happy with what you have because you took action at the right time.

Living out your youth is different than destroying your future. People often think that doing a menial job will disrupt their life or education, but it's actually the opposite. Getting a menial job in high school, tutoring your classmates for a little extra cash, mowing the lawns, shoveling snow, or even opening a lemonade stand over summer vacation are all part of how you get ahead! These jobs are preparing you for the future. You're hustling. Right now, you may only have twenty dollars from five hours of work, but this will convert into two thousand dollars for the same amout time if you just hustle and jostle to get it. So, don't wait for anyone to come and nudge you in the right direction. Work on your résumé, build your portfolio, look for jobs online, make money, and never stop hustling.

Hard work wins.

You get out of life what you put into it. You cannot control a damaging outcome, but you can control the effort expended. Always ask yourself what you could have done to change the outcome. Bad things will happen, but how you deal with them shows the world and yourself where you stand mentally. Never make a negative decision when you're feeling down. Work hard for something you do not care about, and you will constantly be stressed out. Passion comes from working hard on something you love. Do what makes you feel alive, and you'll love what you do.

Invest in yourself.

People consider everything to be undoable until someone actually does it. We discover new things every day, increase our knowledge of the revolving planets, and discern the world's hidden truths. The world is limitless, unending, and incomprehensible in its entirety—and yet, people think they know their limits. The human soul knows no bounds, for it is made of stardust. So why do you think you aren't good enough? Invest in yourself, your time, your thoughts, your energy, and your resources, and strive to become the best version of yourself, excelling at the things other people deem impossible.

Live right now like most people won't, in order to spend the rest of your life like most people can't.

Being broke is a choice—and so is being rich. Entrepreneurs understand that there's an abundance of money in the world. They don't have a "The one-percenters are hoarding all the money" mentality. Entrepreneurship is about moving towards the untouched or uncomfortable, and persevering in the midst of it. When you find a gap in the market, it's because people never thought about it before; therefore, you're the one who will have to bridge that gap. Take advantage of the energy, passion, and wit you have right now and struggle, so you won't have to in the future. Get out of your comfort zone and work hard the first few years, so you can spend the rest of your life like most people can't.

Better five years early than one minute late.

Maybe you realized your dream while working in a nine-to-five job or when you retired from your firm, but it's important to move with alacritous and prompt ardor. You cannot afford to lose a single minute. It's better to work hard and reach your goals early than to be late and let your opportunities slip away. So, study while everyone else is sleeping, work while others are partying, learn while others are procrastinating, and struggle while others are quitting.

You become what you believe.

When it comes to your mindset, think bigger. When it comes to statistics, stop comparing yourself to the average. Rather, understand that there's a spectrum to all statistics and that you're no longer comparing yourself to the average. Don't compare your income to the average income. Comparing yourself to others is the most irrelevant correlation. Be the change in the statistics. Become the example. Become the proof. The difference between a statistic and a success story is you.

If you're only working for the money, you will never make it.

If you're scared of losing money, you won't make any. Money moves life. It is an effective motivator, no doubt about it—but it doesn't last. The greatest minds in the world and the most successful people in every field didn't pursue their careers to make money; their goals were mightier than that. And they made it through because money didn't hold them back, or push them forward. If you make earning money your primary motivation, you will run out of inspiration as soon as you reach your goals. Or perhaps earning enough money will make you comfortable with being miserly. You may not even venture forward, because you'll become *scared of losing* money. Therefore, don't live just to earn money. Rather, improve your skillset and capabilities so that the money comes to you.

PART 2: No Excuses

This section might hit hard for some people, and it may offend some, too. Just know that if these words hit a nerve, there's a reason.

Credit is due when credit is earned.

It is crucial to celebrate the little wins. Not only will it improve your confidence and belief in yourself, it will also improve your prospects for future celebration. You can't celebrate success if you don't acknowledge the grit and perseverance it took to get there. But if you haven't achieved any of your goals and are now sitting idly on the couch, not making any effort, are you really worthy of celebration? The industry doesn't choose based on its own preferences. If you are garnering success and appreciation, you've likely done a good job. But if you aren't, it's not because "the world is out to get you"; it's because you're slacking off.

Increase your efforts, not your excuses.

If you can identify a problem, then you can't use it as an excuse. If you're really serious about changing your outcome, you'll find a way. If not, you'll find an excuse. Stop getting distracted by things that have nothing to do with your goals. People that put in the effort and are eager to follow their passions don't need to make excuses. Those who want to achieve their goals do so with effort and determination. They don't make excuses for themselves, because they know better. Lack of preparation on your end does not constitute an emergency for someone else. If you feel like someone else is holding you back, it's still not an excuse to just let them do it.

The hard truth is that most of the problems in your life are your own fault. Making excuses won't solve them. Your mood, your weight, and your wealth are a reflection of your daily habits. It's on you to get you where you want to be. Take a step, take charge, and put in effort that will pay off.

Your excuse will just come back to bite you, and no one else.

Better to be honest with yourself than to present a lie to others. You may come up with a thousand reasons for not doing something and fool the people around you, but it only takes one person doing what you couldn't to ruin your chances of success. If you keep telling yourself, "I can't do this because _____," know that that is also an excuse. If someone else can, you can too. Don't forget, the difference between who you are and who you want to be is what you do. The only thing stopping you from doing what you want is the story you keep selling yourself as to why you can't.

Those who lack courage will always find a reason to justify it.

You need to realize that there are so many people out there who want it just as bad as you do, if not more. Stop pointing fingers and blaming others for your outcomes. Finding justifications and coming up with reasons to stop working will only hurt you, and nobody else. Self-doubt shatters more dreams than failure does. A lot of things will break your heart, but they will also cure your vision. Strong people break all the time. They just do it quietly, rebuild, and keep on moving forward.

Whatever your excuse is, it's still an *excuse*.

Most people do not truly want freedom, because it involves responsibility. Most people are frightened by responsibility. Anything that starts with "I will get back to it later" or "I can't do it" is an excuse. The "later" never comes, and you end up giving up on the task. It's an excuse. Make the task inescapable. Add an alarm to all your devices, post a note on your fridge or mirror, and tell your family members, friends, or colleagues to remind you. Let it bug you until you do it. This way, you're not perpetuating the habit of giving up or procrastinating.

Be stronger than your excuses.

Maturity is when you realize nobody cares about your excuses. We stand in our own way, then complain that our path is obstructed. Stop defending yourself with destructive ideas, and put aside these so-called "limiting factors" with indefensible logic. Don't blame outside circumstances. Don't choose that easy route. When you complain, you're officially making yourself the victim. Either leave the situation, or change the situation. Around the world, there are people who have done what you only wish you could do. That's all that matters: that someone has done it.

Most people start creating reasons for why they can't achieve something. For instance, "I would have had a better opportunity if..." or "If that hadn't happened, I would have..." and so on. Lying to yourself has already caught up with you. It will only show you where you are mentally. It should be enough to remind you that you are just thinking average.

Your opinion of the world is a reflection of your character.

You're justifying your victim mentality because it's the easiest thing to do. I see a lot of people doing this. They divide each other up into groups, then compare their "oppressions." It is one of the worst things we can do to each other. Take on more responsibility. Take one hundred percent responsibility for your life. More responsibility will also lead to more money. You never know what you're capable of until you're tested. When you take charge of your own life, nothing can stop you—not even yourself.

However, connecting to your mind and body is as necessary as hustling. If you're overworking, your body will find ways to stop you. It may look like the flu, muscle pain, exhaustion, or lack of interest, but it's your body's way of telling you to take a break. You can step back to relax for a while, but come back stronger. Don't stop; take a moment, but don't let it become everlasting. Experiencing a setback doesn't equate to you being a failure. Challenges are growth opportunities. Be stronger than your urge to give up, and don't let setbacks diminish your spark or luster.

The Compound Effect

Your choices determine your success in life—not whatever excuse you have in your head as to why you can't be successful. Compound your thinking, just like money. The same goes for your brain: compound your mentality, and you'll attain a certain mindset/behavior you never thought possible. Just like with investing, decisions compound. Good decisions compound. Bad decisions compound. The best math you can learn is how to calculate the future cost of current decisions.

Financial freedom

Work your nine-to-five job, but make sure you work five-to-nine on yourself. A salary is a drug you receive that makes you forget your dreams. Create a goal by writing your dream down and adding a date. Turn your goal into a plan by breaking it down into steps. Once you back your plan with action, it will become reality. Take time out to work on your future in your present. Formal education can help you make a living, but self-education will make you a fortune. Some of the best education is autodidactic.

Working while others are sleeping will boost your mentality. Retirement is not an age; retirement is when your assets cover your liabilities, and then some. Use your time to make money, then use the money to buy assets, then have the assets to buy yourself time. That's mental and financial freedom. That's how you stay ahead, and that's how you succeed. The relentless pursuit of your goals might mean you sacrifice a few things right now, but it will come back to you twice over in value. You get paid for your value, not your time. The question is, how much do you value yourself?

CHAPTER 5

BE HUMBLE

So, you have achieved your goal, you're living the dream, and you're bathing in pools of cash. What do you do now? You hustle harder and remain humble. People misconstrue material things as a sign of being successful. But they're irrelevant—and most people realize that once they're conveniently obtainable. Society has taught itself to be impressed with stuff that is only impressive to those not worth impressing. Money doesn't change you; it brings out more of who you are. Once you are blessed financially, do not raise your standard of living. Raise your standard of *giving*.

Fear of making a mistake is also a mistake.

Your mistakes improve your understanding. When you see where you went wrong and learn from it, you can mend things and expand your skills. If you go into a new job with the mindset that *I am the best, and nobody can teach me anything,* you're only fooling yourself—and it will destroy your chances of improvement. Everybody in this world—I repeat, *everybody* in this world—has something to offer. Therefore, you can learn from others. So be humble in your beginnings, open your mind and eyes to different perspectives and opinions, and be ready to make mistakes.

It's okay to start slow, and it's okay to grow slow.

The difference between a successful person and a struggling person is their ability to continue. You don't turn into a millionaire overnight. Those who do were also struggling in their past. You don't know how many times they've been kicked to the ground and gotten back up before reaching their destination.

You don't have to be an expert before you get started. It's okay to start small, and it's okay to have humble beginnings. Everyone has flaws. No one is perfect. We're all works in progress. You're collecting wisdom as you go, you're improving your ammo, and you're slowly accelerating towards where you have to be. We're all children deep down; some are more experienced than others. So, it's okay to take baby steps, as long as you don't give up.

Be a brilliant conversationalist, but also be a great listener.

Never interject when a person is talking about their passion. Listen to their words carefully, and try to understand the glow on their face and in their eyes. Some people love the sound of their own voice—so much so that they don't let anyone else talk. Would you like to stay quiet while your colleague talks about their new house or car? I'm sure you'd much rather talk about the things that make you both happy. It's important to listen. In a relationship—with your colleagues, your family, or especially your mind and body—listening is key. A good entrepreneur talks about his/her product or services, but a great one listens to the customer and builds a relationship. That's how you succeed: by being humble and letting others talk. You don't know what's going on in someone else's life. So be kind, don't boast about your blessings, and be humble.

If you are going to a professional for help, tell them your problems, not your solutions. What I mean is that if you're going to a financial advisor, for instance, listen to their advice, and don't interpose with your own opinions to disguise your failure. Most people try to answer their own questions when visiting an expert, either to seem smart, or because they are insecure. Don't be like most people. Let the experts form their opinions based on what you tell them; don't do their job for them. That is how you will get an objective view. To get the best advice, let the expert work to find an answer based on their own experience and perspective. I'm not saying the advice given will be correct, or that you should follow it, but rather, you should understand their viewpoint and act on it on your own merit.

You have to respect yourself before others will respect you.

Being confident is a good way to instill positive energy in yourself. However, when the level of confidence rises above what can be considered standard, that is when everything starts to go down the drain. Confidence isn't about believing that you are better than everyone else; it's realizing that you have no reason to compare yourself to anyone else. It's easy to point out others' mistakes before realizing your own. Similarly, it's easy to find the good in others before you find good in yourself. Here is where most people fail: you have to maintain a balance. Keen observation and the zealous quest to know your true self are your salvation. Point out your mistakes, but also acknowledge your good qualities and successes. That's how you will respect yourself. The positivity and serenity of knowing yourself will attract others to get to know you as well. Be who you are. Approval is not needed; it's what you find within.

People treat you exactly how they feel about you. If you are blind to reality, that's on you. At some point, you must realize that people aren't making mistakes; rather, they are making choices. If you live for others' acceptance, you'll die from their rejections. Be careful what you tolerate, because you're teaching others how they can treat you. Just because someone is on your side doesn't mean they're not playing both sides. At times, people who are in your life only temporarily will teach you permanent lessons. Don't be what others think you are; be your unapologetic true self, and strive to get better. Prove yourself to yourself, not to others.

In the end, you either discipline yourself, or the world does it for you. Take a step forward before it's too late. Hustle and run towards your goals. Don't spend your life chasing your dreams; hunt them, and make no excuses. When you have your goals within your grasp once you are at the finish line, remain humble.

CHAPTER 6

POSITIVE ENERGY

The energy of the mind is the essence of life.
—Aristotle

POSITIVE ENERGY IS MORE THAN just having happy thoughts. It's about maintaining and developing the belief that good things such as success, happiness, health, etc. will come your way. However, the question arises: how can a person do that when they know that they won't be able to amass any wealth in the coming years, because things look so bleak? Well, it might be frowned upon to answer a question with another question, but it fits rather nicely with this scenario: how does a person expect to improve their way of life if they don't ever look past their problems? How does one get past their problems with the mentality that got them there in the first place? Essentially, being positive means anticipating that any obstacle or difficult situation that occurs will eventually work out in your favor in the end.

Hatred is a powerful energy tool and is endlessly renewable.

Hatred cannot be diffused with more hatred. Hate is one energy that has the power to renew itself by feeding on any positive emotion it can find. It is a strong emotion that pollutes the spirit. Know that when you feel like you have done something right, yet people criticize you for it, it is a depiction of their hatred towards you.

Be careful around people that hate in the form of jokes. They're not joking; they're just camouflaging their jealousy. Being jealous of someone's positivity is a form of hatred built around insecurity. Regardless, it has the power to take away your positive energy.

On the other hand, there will be people who hate you no matter what you do. You see, haters know your worth— they just hope you don't. You will never be criticized by someone who is doing more than you, only by those who are doing less. They'll try to tell you all your weak points and hope you fall for their words. There will be many people who secretly compete against you, yet they will still lose. Why? Because their jealousy will engulf the majority of their efforts. Thus, a person who says it cannot be done should not interrupt the person doing it.

Some people only talk about you because they've lost the privilege of talking *with* you. As Albert Einstein correctly described it, "Stay away from negative people. They have a problem for every solution." Hatred, be it within you or towards you, will only destroy you if you adhere to it.

You fail when you stop trying.

This is an extension of what Albert Einstein said: "You never fail until you stop trying." At times, you might feel as if you have failed at everything. However, it doesn't work like that, for you only fail when you give up. Occasionally, it is okay to fall down; what is essential is that you always stand right back up.

Not to be corny, but if you change your vocabulary,

you might have a different perspective. For example, one should never give up after experiencing failure, because "FAIL" means "First Attempt In Learning," and "END" means "Effort Never Dies." Similarly, if someone tells you "NO," remember that it only means "Next Opportunity." Thus, you should always stay positive, regardless of the obstacles.

Don't use your energy to worry.

Thoughts of winning someone over, making your mark in the workplace, proving your worth, etc. are some of the worries that trouble most people today. Being anxious and worrying about the results is only going to drain your energy. Hence, try hard to achieve these goals without worrying about the results too much. However, while things like making your mark in the workplace and getting your project together can be achieved by working harder, the same cannot be said for when you are in a relationship. Just because a relationship has lasted a long time doesn't mean it's working. Worrying and clinging to people who are no longer meant to be in your life is only delaying you from reaching your destiny. This is where you should just stop trying and let them go.

Similarly, if you find yourself arguing with someone and you know you are right, then instead of worrying about proving your stance, allow your mind to be at peace, and give the other person the benefit of the doubt. Walk away from anything that gives you bad vibes. There's no need to explain or make sense of it; it's your life. Be selective in where you place your energy.

However, it's a different criterion when you see someone cutting you off repeatedly even though you are still talking. Never be a pushover for people who tend to take advantage of you. Just as a reminder, knowledge is power, so keep educating yourself.

Every day is a blessing!

This life is a blessing. Every day that you spend in this world, be grateful. If you have a roof over your head, a decent meal to eat, and enough money to educate yourself, consider yourself lucky, for there are many among us who aren't as privileged.

Life is too short to spend it with people who don't make you happy. The less you respond to negative people, the more peaceful your life will become. Choose to sit alone rather than with people who are going to consume your positive energy. Be an inspiration to yourself, because it is within yourself that you have to start from. For a change, sit with the winners. The conversation will be much different than that shared with those of a different mindset.

It is never too early to grow. Set your pace, even if it is slow and steady. What matters is that one should never give up on oneself. Instead of competing with others, start competing with yourself, which will allow you to rise back up each time you encounter failure. Remember that success is a journey, not a destination. It is happiness that you want to pursue throughout your life. Also, if along the way you meet any haters, know that they are your admirers in disguise.

CHAPTER 7

CONCLUSION

Our thoughts and feelings have electromagnetic reality. Manifest wisely.

— Bruce H. Lipton.

EVERYTHING IN THIS WORLD HAS some energy associated with it. If you wish to attain a specific reality, then all you have to do is match the frequency of your thoughts with that particular reality. It is like an investment: the more wisely you invest, the better the outcome will be. However, if you make haste in making your decisions and give way to your negative thoughts, the result is going to be more or less the same. The state of your life is nothing more than a reflection of your state of mind.

Therefore, a lot of your reality depends on what you choose to think.

Reality is fleeting, and it is all in our heads. Nevertheless, the good news is that if it is all in your head, then you have the power to change your reality. Your mindset has the power to determine whether you look at a bad situation and acknowledge it as the worst, or look at the silver lining amidst all the shadows. It is high time that you realize you are responsible for yourself, and it is only you who can decide your own outcome. Nobody else has that power. Hence, you can only be the person you want to be in the future by starting today. There is not enough time in your life to put off becoming who you want to become, so stop delaying your future, because it is not going to lead you anywhere.

Once you start gaining experience, your opinions and perception will automatically change. You will begin to see things from a different perspective and understand them in a better way. It will help you understand yourself and enable you to comprehend the opinions and decisions of other people. Consequently, everything will become easier only if you disconnect yourself from negative energy.

Fear of losing will keep you from winning. However,

when you take risks in pursuit of your desires and dreams, you should know that those risks won't be taken in vain. Even if you lose, there will be something that you will learn from them. Pain is temporary, but regret lasts forever. Face your fears. Then at least in the end, you won't have anything to regret.

Worrying about the future, expecting fast results, anticipating what other people will think, stressing yourself out, overworking, and resisting change are all things that are likely to make you give up on your dreams, which is why it is necessary to keep these fears at bay. So, if any of these fears prevail in your mind, then it is time to increase your power and change your mindset.

Surround yourself with positivity by choosing to sit with people who are intelligent. Surround yourself with people who tell you what you need to hear, not what you *want* to hear. Trust me, this will help you become smarter. You will learn about their objectives and goals, and you will soon reinforce your own in life, because mentality is everything, and the right balance will help you move forward. Initially, it might not seem easy, but with constant practice, you will become better at attaining your goals.

Along the way, you will meet people who criticize

you. You must remember that their perspective doesn't make them right, nor does it make you wrong. In fact, it is recommended that you think differently. Being different is not a problem, as long as it doesn't keep you from looking at the bigger picture. Carve your own path towards your dreams without being afraid of being unique.

There are no physical limitations to achieving your goals, as long as you have the right mentality to support your decisions. It would be best if you reprogrammed your brain to replace wishful thinking with wishful planning. Whether you are going to end up rich or poor solely depends on the direction the scales of your brainpower tilt towards. Similarly to how the stored cache in a computer keeps it from running efficiently, the negative thoughts in your mind are also going to slow you down. Hence, you can always learn from your mistakes without being trapped inside them.

Your mentality is everything, because this is what controls your thoughts, emotions, and actions. It is insanity if you keep doing something over and over and expect a different result each time. Once you start getting repeating results, you should know that the approach needs to be changed. What is vital for success is that you change your mentality and adapt to change according to the environment. Consume positive material, because it is only when people think positively that they are able to manifest and attract positivity in their lives. Success will find its way to you if you strengthen your mind and take that first step. Success is rented, and you'll need to put in the work consistently. If you stop, it will slowly fade.

Review your mistakes, make the right choice, sustain your success, and play it smart without submitting to your failure. Instead of complaining, get back up and give yourself another chance. You will be surprised, because that is the key to success. If you are going to excel in everything that you do, then you must set your mind to it. Believe me, stepping back from your problems is only going to delay your destiny. Try to find your way out of any negative situation. Every problem has a solution; all you have to do is to focus.

Perspective is everything. In order to shape your future, you must shape your perspective first. Whether you notice the positivity or gloom over the negativity, it is completely in your own hands. So choose wisely, because your perspective will either help you move forward or hold you back.

The viewpoints, opinions, and mindset that you

garner are the determining factors in how you look at a situation. Choosing to look at the positive side of things will remove the unhelpful, unconstructive pessimism and negativity from your life. Before these thoughts can meddle with your brain, take a deep breath and work on being productive. Life is not a bed of roses, and anyone who tells you otherwise probably doesn't want you to flourish. Life is a constant struggle, and all good things take time. Don't give up on your failures; keep working on the solutions.

Challenge your thinking by keeping your mind open. Continuously learn. Instead of criticizing, compliment. Instead of fearing change, embrace it. Nothing is free, and no one owes you anything. Instead of blaming others for your failures, take responsibility. New goals require new habits. You can't change what you've done, but you can change what you're doing.

When it's time for you to go, will you look back and see yourself as the person you expected to become? Questions like this should help you evaluate your current situation in terms of whether or not you're making the right decisions today. This will lead you to become the person you wish to be. The price must be paid now for the process to follow.

Usually, starting is what stops most people. You have enough time; you just need to adjust your priorities. If you see yourself in a bad environment or situation, get yourself out of it as soon as possible. Don't be a product of your environment; be a product of your choices. Don't disrespect yourself by saying "yes" to plans you really want to (and should) say "no" to. Don't let anyone guilt-trip you into doing things you don't want to. Avoid the people that bring out the person you no longer wish to be.

Are you trying to be comfortable, or are you trying to grow? You can't do both. You can't give your life more time, so give your time more life. Be kind to yourself and others. Be silent when you're angry. Never show weakness. Be calm in every situation. Instead of holding grudges, forgive. Take nothing personally. Life is beautiful. Appreciate everything you have. Be confident with who you are, and extend love, happiness, and peace to yourself and others. You are your best friend. Be everything for yourself.

In the future, you'll be more disappointed by the things you didn't do than by the things you *did* do. Therefore, discover your own entelechy.

ACKNOWLEDGMENT

I want to thank my parents, Maria and Manny Paloumbis.